DATE DUE

American Symbols
AND THEIR **Meanings**

THE
BALD
EAGLE

American Symbols
AND THEIR Meanings

THE
BALD
EAGLE

HAL MARCOVITZ

MASON CREST PUBLISHERS
PHILADELPHIA

Copyright © 2003 by Mason Crest Publishers. All rights reserved. Printed and bound in the Hashemite Kingdom of Jordan.

First printing

1 3 5 7 9 8 6 4 2

Library of Congress Cataloging-in-Publication Data on file at the Library of Congress

ISBN 1-59084-032-1

American Symbols
AND THEIR **Meanings**

CONTENTS

The Importance of American Symbols

Symbols are not merely ornaments to admire—they also tell us stories. If you look at one of them closely, you may want to find out why it was made and what it truly means. If you ask people who live in the society in which the symbol exists, you will learn some things. But by studying the people who created that symbol and the reasons why they made it, you will understand the deepest meanings of that symbol.

The United States owes its identity to great events in history, and the most remarkable American Symbols are rooted in these events. The struggle for independence from Great Britain gave America the Declaration of Independence, the Liberty Bell, the American flag, and other images of freedom. The War of 1812 gave the young country a song dedicated to the flag, "The Star-Spangled Banner," which became our national anthem. Nature gave the country its national animal, the bald eagle. These symbols established the identity of the new nation, and set it apart from the nations of the Old World.

To be emotionally moving, a symbol must strike people with a sense of power and unity. But it often takes a long time for a new symbol to be accepted by all the people, especially if there are older symbols that have gradually lost popularity. For example, the image of Uncle Sam has replaced Brother Jonathan, an earlier representation of the national will, while the Statue of Liberty has replaced Columbia, a woman who represented liberty to Americans in the early 19th century. Since then, Uncle Sam and the Statue of Liberty have endured and have become cherished icons of America.

Of all the symbols, the Statue of Liberty has perhaps the most curious story, for unlike other symbols, Americans did not create her. She was created by the French, who then gave her to America. Hence, she represented not what Americans thought of their country but rather what the French thought of America. It was many years before Americans decided to accept this French goddess of Liberty as a symbol for the United States and its special role among the nations: to spread freedom and enlighten the world.

This series of books is valuable because it presents the story of each of America's great symbols in a freshly written way and will contribute to the students' knowledge and awareness of them. It is to be hoped that this information will awaken an abiding interest in American history, as well as in the meanings of American symbols.

—*Barry Moreno,*
librarian and historian
Ellis Island/Statue of Liberty National Monument

The Apollo 11 lunar module (LM) *Eagle* above the moon's surface, as seen in a photo taken by command module pilot Michael Collins. Because of the importance of their historic mission, the astronauts had decided to use the eagle as the name for the ship that would land on the moon. The inset shows the members of the Apollo 11 crew: Neil Armstrong, Michael Collins, and Edwin "Buzz" Aldrin.

"THE *EAGLE* HAS LANDED"

The tiny spacecraft drifted over the surface of the Moon. Below, a stark gray landscape stretched out in all directions. **Astronauts** Neil Armstrong and Buzz Aldrin were searching for a place to make a soft landing away from the rocks, boulders, and sharp ridges that dominated the terrain.

Back on Earth, Mission Control in Houston radioed the astronauts: *"Eagle,* you're go for landing." *Eagle* was the name Armstrong, Aldrin, and astronaut Michael Collins had given to the lunar module. Collins was not aboard *Eagle;* he was orbiting overhead in the command module, which the astronauts had named *Columbia.*

It was July 20, 1969. Four days earlier, the three astronauts had blasted off from Cape Canaveral in Florida aboard Apollo 11. The mission of Apollo 11 was to land two astronauts on the Moon and return them safely to Earth. If successful, Armstrong and Aldrin would become the first men to walk on the Moon.

Earlier Apollo missions had been test runs. On one previous mission, the astronauts had named the command module *Gumdrop* and the lunar module *Spider*. It was easy to see why. Flat on the bottom and curving up to a blunt point, the command module resembled a gumdrop; meanwhile, the fragile lunar module was not much more than a small cabin supported by four skinny legs, giving it the definite appearance of a spider. Another Apollo mission employed the names *Charlie Brown* and *Snoopy*, characters from the newspaper comic strip "Peanuts," for the command and lunar modules.

While Collins was amused by such names, he knew similar names would never do for Apollo 11. "We felt Apollo 11 was no ordinary flight and we wanted no ordinary design," recalled Collins.

The shoulder patch worn by the Apollo 11 astronauts shows an eagle bearing a palm branch—a sign of peace—landing on the moon.

It was Jim Lovell, a backup pilot for Apollo 11, who first suggested "eagle" for the mission. Collins found a book on birds and turned to a page showing an image of a bald eagle—feet extended, wings partially folded, preparing to land. Collins made a rough sketch of an eagle landing on a cratered lunar surface, and the emblem for Apollo 11 was born. "The choice of an eagle as a motif for the landing led swiftly to naming the landing craft itself *Eagle*," Collins said.

* * *

At just over a mile above the lunar surface, with Armstrong at the controls of *Eagle*, problems arose. The rocky lunar surface was making it difficult to land, and the *Eagle* was running low on fuel. It seemed likely the astronauts would have to abort the mission. Suddenly, Armstrong found a break in a boulder field. The *Eagle* flew over a smooth and flat area on the eastern edge of the area called the Sea of Tranquility. As he eased the *Eagle* gently toward the lunar surface, the spacecraft was engulfed in a cloud of dust kicked up by the exhaust from its engine.

A light flashed on the *Eagle*'s control panel, telling the astronauts that a probe on the bottom of the Lunar Module had touched the lunar surface. "We copy you down, *Eagle*," said Mission Control in Houston. A few seconds passed. And then, a voice from the Moon.

"Houston, Tranquility Base here," Armstrong said. "The *Eagle* has landed."

Bald eagles have great eyesight. Their eyes are four to eight times sharper than a human's. The bald eagle can be found in a variety of habitats, from rugged, forested Arctic coasts to the dry, hot deserts of the Baja peninsula in northern Mexico. In the wild, bald eagles may live 25 years or longer; captive birds have lived as long as 47 years.

LIKE A THUNDER-BOLT

*W*hen astronauts Armstrong, Aldrin, and Collins named their lunar spacecraft *Eagle*, they selected a bird that had represented the spirit of America for some 200 years.

Other cultures far older than America's had admired eagles as well. In Greek mythology, the eagle was said to represent the god Zeus. In ancient Rome, images of eagles were emblazoned on the shields of warriors. Over the centuries, rulers in France, Germany, Russia, and Austria-Hungary adopted eagles as their symbols.

The birds revered by warriors, kings, and poets were golden eagles. They are large, fierce birds with mostly

The inside of this Greek cup is decorated with an image of the god Zeus and an eagle. In mythology, Zeus was represented by an eagle, and the ancient Greeks considered the birds sacred.

dark brown feathers, although the feathers near the backs of their heads and necks are golden, giving the species its name. Golden eagles are found in Europe, North America, Africa, and Australia, mostly in mountainous regions.

They are cousins of the American bald eagles, which are known as sea eagles because they are fish eaters. Bald eagles were originally found along America's coasts, although in recent years bird counters have spotted bald eagles in all states except Hawaii.

When European settlers arrived in America in the late 1600s and early 1700s, they found many bald eagles. Early bird watchers reported finding at least one nest of eagles for every mile of coastline along the Chesapeake Bay. Eagles were also extremely abundant along the Hudson River in New York and the coast of Maine.

Adult females are larger than adult males. The female grows to a length of 35 to 37 inches; the male is slightly shorter, usually between 30 and 34 inches. Female wingspan reaches from 79 to 96 inches, while the male wingspan stretches from 72 to 85 inches. Bald eagles weigh between eight and 15 pounds.

Eagles have been known to live as long as 47 years in captivity, but the average lifespan is believed to be about 15 to 20 years.

Eagles' feathers are *down*-lined, making the birds tolerant to cold. An adult eagle has 7,000 feathers and they help keep the bird warm by trapping layers of air. An eagle can maintain an even body temperature by simply ruffling its feathers. To sun itself on a cold morning, the eagle will ruffle its feathers so that the air pockets are open.

The voice of the eagle is shrill and high-pitched. It is believed that bald eagles communicate to show their affection to one another, and to make warnings that *predators* are nearby.

Eagles court much the same way humans do—they show off in front of one another. Late-winter breeding season in eagle country usually features many displays of fast, intricate, and

> According to an ancient Aztec legend, the eagle and the jaguar fought over the honor of becoming the sun; the eagle settled the matter by flinging himself into fire, thus becoming the sun.

exhilarating flying skills. Bird watchers have reported seeing eagles courting in an amazing high-speed maneuver, the two birds swooping at each other in barrel rolls while they somehow manage to avoid a collision. The maneuver ends when the two eagles lock *talons*, then fall toward earth spinning like a cartwheel, releasing each other just a few feet above the ground, where they zoom back into the sky to do it all again.

Once they mate, eagles will remain together as a couple until one of them dies. The surviving spouse will then seek a new mate.

Eagles build nests in trees or along rocky ledges. They are composed of sticks but lined with moss, feathers, fur, and plants. Once a pair of eagles builds a nest, they will likely maintain it for several years, although it will be constantly repaired or rebuilt during each nesting season. One nest bird watchers kept an eye on stayed intact for 34 years. Nests can also become very large—as much as seven or eight feet across.

Bald eagle eggs are a dull white, somewhat darker than a chicken's egg. Once laid, an eagle egg will hatch in 34 or 35 days. Males and females are known to share the *incubation* chores equally, although the female always seems to be around when the eggs hatch. Food is brought to the nest by both parents, but the female will take care of feeding the baby eaglets.

Bald eagles are fish eaters and they will swim, briefly; they use an overhand motion with their wings that is similar to the butterfly stroke. If fish are not available they'll look for other birds, small rodents, and even larger animals.

If eggs are laid several days apart and one egg hatches before another, the

The bald eagle is, of course, not bald. The name stems from the word "piebald," which means a place of black and white patches. That description roughly fits the bald eagle, whose head, neck, and tail feathers are white, while his remaining feathers are blackish-brown. There are no other birds in North America with white heads and tails. The beak of the bald eagle is hooked, which helps it tear flesh away from the body of its kill.

first-hatched eaglet has a jump on his nest-mate. With one eaglet growing ahead of the other, the larger baby usually begins to take advantage of his little brother or sister, often pecking at it to keep it from getting its share of food. Often, the smaller eaglet is killed by its older nest-mate or dies from starvation. The parents do nothing to help the younger bird.

Baby eaglets begin standing on their own feet at about three weeks of age. By six weeks of age, they weigh about eight pounds and have started growing their own feathers. By eight weeks, they are able to feed themselves with the food their parents bring to the nest.

Bald eagles don't come by their distinctive **plumage** until they are four or five years old. Younger birds have a mix of brown and white feathers.

As they grow more feathers, they spend more time grooming themselves. They are also prancing around the nest, exercising their wings and testing them by making flapping motions.

Finally, sometime around the tenth week after its birth, the young eagle stands on the edge of the nest, faces into a strong wind, flaps its wings and takes its first tentative flight aloft. The young eagle won't go far at first, and initial solo flights are usually bumpy and accident-prone.

The young eagles will take practice flights farther and farther from the nest for the next month or so. During this period, they start relying less on their parents to find food and more on their own hunting skills. Soon, they will leave the nest and strike out on their own.

Adult eagles are expert flyers, preferring to stay aloft by gliding along on air currents. Their wings are long and broad, making them perfect for soaring. Eagles use "thermals" to stay aloft. These are rising currents of warm air. Eagles are also very good at finding updrafts created by the mountainous landscape to give them a boost upward. By taking advantage of air currents, eagles find they can fly without flapping their wings very often, which means they can stay aloft for long periods of time by expending little energy.

Their tails help them soar. While gliding, the eagle's tail feathers are spread in order to create a large surface to catch the thermals and updrafts. Tails also help the eagles slow down for a landing, a dive, or a swoop toward *prey.*

When eagles are on long-distance migratory flights, they climb high in a thermal, then glide downward searching for another thermal. The eagles continue to ride the warm air currents until they get to where they want to go.

THE GREAT SEAL OF THE UNITED STATES

Much thought went into designing the seal of the United States. After members of the Second Continental Congress signed the Declaration of Independence on July 4, 1776, they turned their attention to creating a seal, which would be used to represent the nation on official documents.

A NEW NATION EMERGES

merica's founding fathers decided their new nation would need a Great Seal on July 4, 1776, the same day they voted to adopt the Declaration of Independence. The Continental *Congress* considered the Great Seal a matter of importance and appointed Benjamin Franklin, Thomas Jefferson, and John Adams to a committee charged with the responsibility "to bring in a device for a seal for the United States of America."

A seal is a symbol used to mark a document, giving it a degree of authenticity. The seal of the government marks a document as official. In other words, any document containing the government's seal proves that

The scientific name for the bald eagle is *Haliaeetus leucocephalus*; it is the only species of sea eagle living in the United States. Other sea eagles live in Europe, Asia, Africa and Australia.

the document carries the weight and authority of the government behind it. The founding fathers regarded it as vitally important that their new nation have its own official seal—a Great Seal—to be stamped onto all papers showing that the government of the United States had the authority to pass laws and issue orders. At the time, America was facing war with Great Britain. Clearly, the founding fathers knew that any actions their new government would be taking to fight the war had to carry the Great Seal of the United States.

Seals are sometimes fixed to a document by a printer. Sometimes they are fixed to the document by a stamp that makes an impression of the image right into the paper. In the days of the Continental Congress, the seal was often cast into a metal die and pressed into hot wax that was dripped onto the document.

Franklin worked on a design and produced a scene from the Bible. Franklin's idea for the Great Seal included an image of a crowned pharaoh pursuing the Israelites through the divided waters of the Red Sea. On the opposite shore stood the figure of Moses, bathed in light and extending his arms toward the sea, ordering the waters to close on pharaoh and his chariots. Surrounding that image were the words: "Rebellion

Against Tyranny is Obedience to God." Obviously, Ben Franklin considered the plight of the colonists in America to be similar to the flight from Egyptian slavery experienced by the Israelites in biblical times.

Neither Jefferson nor Adams agreed with the design. Jefferson suggested moving the Israelites to the wilderness, where they could be shown searching for their homeland. He did endorse the motto, though, and later used Franklin's words on his personal seal, which he stamped on papers at his home in Virginia.

Adams had a totally different idea. He suggested an image of the Greek hero Hercules being tested by female figures in the roles of Virtue and Vice. In Adams' image, Vice would lure Hercules to the path of self-indulgence while Virtue would urge Hercules to climb the rugged hill of duty and honor.

None of those ideas were accepted by the Continental Congress, which decided to appoint a second committee to design the Great Seal.

This committee was headed by three members of the Congress: James Lovell of Massachusetts, John Morin Scott of New York, and William Churchill Houston of New Jersey. The committee, which formed on March 25, 1780, sought the help of artist Francis Hopkinson of Philadelphia, who had signed the Declaration of

> **The bald eagle can fly up to 40 miles an hour in normal flight, and can dive at speeds of more than 100 miles an hour.**

Charles Thomson was respected by the Native Americans in colonial Pennsylvania. In fact, when he was 29, the Delaware Indians adopted him as a member of the tribe and gave him a name that meant "Man-Who-Talks-the-Truth."

In 1774, Thomson was appointed secretary of the Continental Congress, where he earned his reputation for demanding that all reports issued by Congress contain nothing but the truth. When a congressional report was issued under his signature, this expression was often heard: "Here comes the truth."

Independence and designed the American flag.

Hopkinson produced a drawing of a shield decorated by 13 red and white stripes supported on one side by a warrior holding a sword and on the other by a figure holding an olive branch, representing "Peace." Above the shield shone a *constellation* of 13 stars. Hopkinson suggested a motto in Latin that said: *Bello vel Paci,* which means "For War or for Peace."

That version was rejected as well.

Once more, the Continental Congress appointed a committee to design the Great Seal. This time, the committee was composed of Charles Thomson, the secretary of the Congress, and two members of the Congress, Arthur Lee and Elias Boudinot. To help compose the seal, Thomson asked for help from William Barton, a writer and attorney. It was Barton who first raised the idea of adding the image of a bald eagle to the seal.

"The eagle displayed is the symbol of supreme power and authority and signifies the Congress," Barton wrote. "Being placed on the summit of the column, it is emblematical of the sovereignty of the government of the United States."

Barton made other recommendations for the seal. He suggested the image include a sword, an American flag, a pillar, a dove, a woman dressed in a gown of glittering stars and crown, and a constellation of 13 stars.

Thomson took Barton's ideas, added some of his own, and produced the final design for the Great Seal. Under Thomson's design, the most prominent figure in the emblem was the eagle. Thomson specified that it be an "American eagle on the wing and rising."

William Barton worked with Charles Thomson to make the eagle a part of the Great Seal of the United States.

The eldest of 10 children, Barton grew up in Philadelphia and studied law in England, returning just before the 13 colonies declared their independence from Great Britain. After the war, he worked as an attorney and writer. One of his books was a biography of his uncle, the astronomer David Rittenhouse.

It is likely that Barton and Thomson met as members of the American Philosophical Society, an organization Thomson helped to found, which would go on to serve as a place where members could exchange ideas about independence and democracy.

Benjamin Franklin, one of the most important early American leaders, did not
want to use the bald eagle as the
national symbol. Instead, he wanted
to use a turkey on the Great Seal.
Franklin wrote:

> I wish the bald eagle had not been cho-
> sen as the representative of our country.
> He is a bird of bad moral character, he
> does not get his living honestly, you may have
> seen him perched on some dead tree, where, too
> lazy to fish for himself, he watches the labor of the fishing-
> hawk, and when that diligent bird has at length taken a fish,
> and is bearing it to its nest for the support of his mate and
> young ones, the bald eagle pursues him and takes it from
> him. Besides, he is a rank coward; the little kingbird, not big-
> ger than a sparrow, attacks him boldly and drives him out of
> the district. He is therefore by no means a proper emblem
> for a brave and honest America. The turkey in comparison is
> a much more respectable bird and a true native of America
> ... a bird of courage, and would not hesitate to attack a
> grenadier of the British guards, who should presume to
> invade his farmyard with a red coat on.

Next, he placed a shield of stars and stripes across the breast of the eagle and incorporated arrows and an olive branch into the design to show "the power of peace and war." In the eagle's beak, he placed a banner with the Latin words *E Pluribus Unum,* meaning, "Out of Many, One."

Above the eagle's head Thomson placed a silver constellation of 13 stars. He wrote, "The constellation denotes a new state taking its place and rank among the sovereign powers. The shield is born on the breast of the American eagle without any other supporters, to denote that the United States of America ought to rely on their own Virtue."

On June 20, 1782, Congress accepted the design but not without some dissent. Ben Franklin was a major opponent of the eagle. He insisted on a turkey! Nevertheless, Congress preferred the eagle and ordered the die cast for the new Great Seal of the United States.

As the figure carved at the top of this totem pole shows, the eagle has been an important American symbol since long before Europeans arrived here in the 16th and 17th centuries. Native Americans held the eagle sacred, and warriors were only allowed to wear eagle feathers when they had performed feats the tribe considered exceptionally brave.

A SYMBOL IN AMERICA

The bald eagle was a symbol in America long before it was America's symbol. For centuries before white settlers arrived on their lands, Native Americans had adopted the eagle as a symbol of bravery, painting its image on their shields and using eagle feathers in their headdresses and to guide their arrows.

Many great chiefs and warriors made "Eagle" part of their names. They included Kill Eagle, a leader of the Blackfoot Sioux Indians who fought against General George Custer at the Battle of the Little Big Horn in Montana. Others included Big Eagle, a Santee Sioux chief in Minnesota; White Eagle, chief of the Ponca

Indians in Nebraska, and Eagle Heart, chief of the Kiowa Indians in Oklahoma.

Sadly, those chiefs made their names fighting against soldiers of the U.S. Army during the Indian wars in the second half of the 19th century. Yellow Eagle, for example, was a fierce Oglala Sioux warrior who killed many *cavalry* soldiers.

Although Indian society and culture in America was largely wiped out by the end of the 19th century, the image of the eagle lived on to inspire others. In 1933, millions of Americans were out of work. Many families were hungry and homeless. The era was known as the Great *Depression*. To help the economy recover and put men back to work, the new president, Franklin D. Roosevelt, conceived the National Industrial Recovery Act—a law that would spend billions of dollars on public works projects. New bridges, roads and government buildings were constructed under contracts approved by the National Recovery Administration (NRA), the agency Roosevelt set up to administer the program and hire workers from the ranks of the unemployed.

For its symbol, the National Recovery Administration selected the eagle. For years, the NRA's blue eagle was a familiar symbol to hard-working Americans. They owed their jobs and the food on their tables to the government agency represented by the eagle with wings spread wide, lightning bolts held in the talons of one foot, a mechanical gear held in the other.

National Recovery Administration posters, featuring the agency's eagle logo, could be seen in the windows of businesses during the 1930s

The National Recovery Administration was neither the first agency of the government nor the last to make use of the eagle in its official emblem. The eagle appears in the seal of the president of the United States as well as the Supreme Court. Cabinet agencies that have adopted the eagle into their seals include the Defense, Commerce,

Justice, Labor, and State Departments. Other government agencies that employ the eagle in their seals are the Central Intelligence Agency, National Labor Relations Board, Social Security Administration, Library of Congress, Patent Office, and dozens more.

The jobs of these agencies are hardly similar—the Central Intelligence Agency is responsible for gathering information about unfriendly foreign governments, often through the use of spies, while the Social Security Administration is charged with collecting money from workers' paychecks to hold for their retirement years. And yet, both agencies feel the bald eagle represents the spirit that enables them to carry out their missions.

The American military has long employed the image of an eagle to adorn its medals, decorations, and insignias on uniforms. The eagle appears on the Congressional Medal of Honor—the highest medal awarded for bravery to American soldiers and sailors.

For decades, images of the eagle have appeared on the "tails" side of American coins. In fact, after the Moon landing in 1969, the U.S. Bureau of the Mint issued dollar coins showing an eagle with wings spread, coming in for a landing on the lunar surface. The image is similar to the design astronaut Michael Collins conceived shortly before the blastoff of Apollo 11. In addition to coins, the eagle has also shown up on paper money and on stamps issued by the U.S. Postal Service.

> Today the symbol for the Republican Party in America is the elephant, but when the party formed in 1854, its leaders adopted the eagle as the party's first symbol.

During the War of 1812, the flag aboard the *Lawrence*, the ship of Commodore Matthew Perry, depicted a flying eagle with a banner held in its beak. The banner said: "Don't Give Up the Ship." During the Battle of Lake Erie, the *Lawrence* began to sink; Perry transferred the flag to the ship *Niagara* and continued the fight.

Eagles show up in the symbols of state governments as well. You can find the image of the eagle in the state flags or seals of Alabama, Illinois, Michigan, Mississippi, New Mexico, New York, North Dakota, Oregon, Pennsylvania, and Utah.

If the government can make use of the eagle, others can as well. A professional athletic team that adopted the bald eagle as its symbol is the Philadelphia Eagles of the National Football League. In fact, the team's founders

In 1909, William D. Boyce was having trouble finding an address in Chicago, Illinois, when a young boy approached him and asked Boyce if he could be of help. The boy was familiar with the neighborhood and led Boyce to the address. That act of kindness by the young stranger prompted Boyce to found the Boy Scouts of America a year later.

Now, some 5 million boys are members of the Boy Scouts of America. A few of them go on to become Eagle Scouts—the highest rank in the organization, and one that can only be achieved after years of dedicated service to scouting. Since 1910, about 1 million boys have earned the rank of Eagle Scout.

To become an Eagle Scout, a boy must display leadership and perform service to his community. Some famous Eagle Scouts are former President Gerald R. Ford, astronauts Neil Armstrong and James Lovell, Supreme Court Justice Stephen Breyer, film director Steven Spielberg, author Harrison Salisbury, former U.S. Senator Bill Bradley, Olympic athlete Willie Banks, and H. Ross Perot, a businessman and one-time presidential candidate.

said they were inspired to use the name in support of the National Recovery Administration. The 1984 Olympic Organizing Committee in Los Angeles adopted a cartoon eagle as a mascot for the Olympic Games held that year in Southern California. The character's name was Sam Eagle, and he wore a tall red, white, and blue top hat, similar to the hat worn by Uncle Sam.

Airplane manufacturers and airlines were quick to adopt the eagle as a symbol. American Airlines, for example, depicts an eagle with raised wings in its *logo*. Other corporations have been happy to make use of the eagle, too. The American Thread Company, for one, started using the eagle to help it sell yarn in 1863.

In 1898, a group of six theater owners in Seattle, Washington, decided to form a social club they named "The Order of Good Things." After several meetings, they adopted the eagle as their emblem and changed their name to the *"Fraternal Order of Eagles."* Soon, the organization spread to other cities and the Fraternal Order of Eagles became a

> **The rock music group The Eagles has sold 90 million albums since forming in 1971.**

national association. Presidents of the United States who belonged to the Fraternal Order of Eagles included Theodore Roosevelt, Warren G. Harding, Franklin Roosevelt, Harry Truman, John F. Kennedy, and Jimmy Carter. Today, there are more than 1.1 million members of the Fraternal Order of Eagles. One of the greatest contributions of the Fraternal Order of Eagles was Mother's Day; it was first proposed by Eagles member Frank E. Hering in 1904.

Although the bald eagle had been an important American symbol for hundreds of years,
by the 1970s the birds were nearly extinct in
the continental United States. Over the last
25 years, bald eagles have made a comeback;
In 2001, the population of bald eagles in the
lower 48 states was estimated at 20,000, with
another 35,000 eagles living in Alaska.

SAVING OUR PROUDEST SYMBOL

*W*hen the settlers from Europe first arrived on
American shores, it is believed that some
500,000 bald eagles were alive and thriving in the New
World. But the vast country soon proved too small for
men and eagles. As the population of America grew, the
species of the bald eagle was nearly wiped out.

Even after the eagle was named a national symbol,
eagles were regarded as *vermin*—to be shot on sight.
This was due to the eagles' feeding habits. When fishing
was poor, the eagles would fly inland in search of food,
often eating the *carcasses* of dead animals.

By 1940, Congress first realized that Americans were

wiping out the national bird. Members of Congress adopted the "Bald Eagle Protection Act," which made it unlawful for people to kill eagles or disturb their eggs.

Still, the species continued to decline. Why? The answer was eventually found on the nation's farm fields. A chemical called **DDT** had been used for decades to kill insects that feed on farm crops. But after a heavy rain, the DDT drained into nearby streams and rivers. The fish swimming in the streams ingested the DDT. Later, the fish were eaten by the eagles. When the eagles ate the DDT-infected fish, the chemicals from the *insecticide* entered the eagles' bodies.

By the 1960s, scientists found that DDT poisoning had caused eagle egg shells to become very brittle. They cracked under the weight of the mother warming the eggs. The DDT often affected the birds as well, killing them at young ages or killing the baby eagles still in the shells. Ospreys, pelicans, and other birds that feed on fish were also affected.

The *zoologist* who made the dangers of DDT known to the public was Rachel Carson, who wrote extensively on the effects of the insecticide on wildlife in her 1962 book, *Silent Spring*. The book told how fewer eagles were living on the western coast of Florida. "Between 1952 and 1957, about 80 percent of the nests failed to produce young. In the last year of this period only 43 nests were occupied," Carson wrote. "Seven of them produced young (eight eaglets); 23 contained eggs that failed to

Rachel Carson grew up in the rural town of Springdale, Pennsylvania. In 1929, she graduated from Chatham College with a degree in marine biology. Early in her career, she was able to combine a love for writing with her work in zoology by writing articles on natural history and conservation for the *Baltimore Sun* newspaper. Later, she became an editor of publications for the U.S. Fish and Wildlife Service.

In 1941, Carson published her first book, *Under the Sea-Wind*. Ten years later, her second book, *The Sea Around Us*, became an international best-seller and established Carson as an important voice for environmental protection. But it was *Silent Spring* (1962) that became her most important book. Her warnings about the dangers of DDT prompted the U.S. Environmental Protection Agency to ban the use of the insecticide in 1972.

Rachel Carson died of breast cancer in 1964.

hatch; 13 were used merely as feeding stations by adult eagles and contained no eggs."

Carson also studied the eagle population at Hawk Mountain, a bird *sanctuary* in Pennsylvania. She wrote: "During the first years after the sanctuary was established, from 1935 to 1939, 40 percent of the eagles were yearlings. But in recent years these immature birds have become a rarity. Between 1955 and 1959, they made up only 20 percent of the total count, and in one year, 1957, there were only one young eagle for every 32 adults."

By 1963, it was believed that only 417 breeding pairs of bald eagles existed in the lower 48 states. Americans had nearly wiped out their national bird. Carson blamed DDT. She called it "an elixir of death."

The plight of the bald eagle was not totally hopeless. Eagles continued to thrive in the wilderness of Alaska. Nevertheless, steps had to be taken to protect the eagles on the mainland. By the mid-1970s, it was believed that just a single pair of eagles was alive in the state of New York. In 1977, just 32 pairs of eagles existed in the Chesapeake Bay region. Blood samples taken at that time from eagles in Maine showed the birds continued to carry traces of DDT—the insecticide was being passed down in the birds from generation to generation.

Despite this, the government was slow to protect the bald eagle. In 1972, the U.S. Environmental Protection Agency banned the use of DDT. The next year, Congress adopted the Endangered Species Act, which protects any species of animal that in danger of being wiped out. The American bald eagle was placed on the list of endangered species in 1978. In fact, the eagle was listed as "on the brink of extinction" that year by the U.S. Fish and Wildlife Service.

About 20,000 American bald eagles live in the Canadian province of British Columbia.

Once placed on the endangered species list, the eagles were protected by tough federal laws designed to safeguard both the birds and their habitats. It now became illegal to build houses, businesses, factories, roads, bridges, or anything else in places where eagles lived.

Congress also gave the Fish and Wildlife Service money to breed eagles in captivity. They would then release the healthy birds in areas where the species had disappeared.

Those activities worked. In 1994, the Fish and Wildlife Service announced that the population of eagles in the lower 48 states had grown to 4,000 pairs. The agency proposed that the bald eagle be taken off the endangered species list and classified as a "threatened species." As a threatened species, bald eagles would

> A big threat to the survival of eagles now is lead poisoning. The birds sometimes eat deer and ducks that had been killed, but lost, by hunters. The eagles ingest the lead rifle shots.

still be protected under federal law. However, money would be diverted from breeding eagles to breeding other species on the endangered list.

On July 2, 1999, in a ceremony at the White House, President Bill Clinton formally proposed the bald eagle removed from the endangered species list. "The American bald eagle is now back from the brink of extinction, thriving in virtually every state of the union," Clinton said. "I can think of no better way to honor the birth of our nation than by celebrating the rebirth of our proudest living symbol."

1776 On July 4, the day the Continental Congress adopts the Declaration of Independence, the new nation's lawmakers appoint Benjamin Franklin, Thomas Jefferson, and John Adams to a committee to design the Great Seal of the United States.

1780 A committee that includes Charles Thomson, Arthur Lee, Elias Boudinot, and William Barton comes up with the concept of including a bald eagle on the Great Seal of the United States.

1782 On June 20, Congress adopts the Great Seal of the United States, which features the image of an eagle, despite the protests of Benjamin Franklin, who wanted to use the wild turkey on the seal instead.

1904 Fraternal Order of Eagles member Frank E. Hering proposes a national day honoring mothers known as "Mother's Day."

1933 The National Recovery Administration takes as its symbol a blue eagle, clutching a gear in one claw and lightning bolts in the other.

1940 Congress passes the Bald Eagle Protection Act, making it illegal to harm eagles or disturb their eggs.

1962 *Silent Spring* by Rachel Carson is published, calling attention to the effect on eagles and other animals by the insecticide DDT.

1963 Just 417 breeding pairs of eagles are believed living in the lower 48 states.

1969 The Apollo 11 lunar module named *Eagle* lands on the Moon.

1972 U.S. Environmental Protection Agency bans the use of DDT.

1973 Congress adopts the U.S. Endangered Species Act.

1978 Bald eagles are classified as an endangered species.

1984 Sam the Eagle is the mascot for the Olympic Games, held in Los Angeles.

1988 2,000 breeding pairs of eagles reported in the United States.

1992 3,700 breeding pairs and 7,500 juvenile eagles reported in the continental United States, bringing the population of bald eagles outside Alaska to nearly 15,000.

1994 After reporting 4,000 breeding pairs in the lower 48 states, U.S. Fish and Wildlife Service declares the eagle is no longer an endangered species.

2001 The population of the Bald Eagle is estimated at 20,000 in the lower 48 states, with another 20,000 eagles living in British Columbia and 35,000 in Alaska. The eagle is expected to be taken off the threatened species list, and reclassified as "fully recovered."

astronaut—a person trained to fly missions in space.

carcass—the body of a dead animal.

cavalry—a group of soldiers who go into battle on horseback.

Congress—the lawmaking branch of the United States government.

constellation—a group of stars that form a familiar pattern in the night sky.

DDT—a chemical substance that until the 1960s was used to kill insects that feed on farm crops; the complete scientific name is dichloro-diphenyl-trichloroethane.

depression—a period during which business is slow, forcing many people into unemployment. The Great Depression lasted from 1929 until the late 1930s.

down—a soft and thick layer of feathers which can be found closest to the skin of a bird.

fraternal—men in a brotherly union.

incubation—the period during which baby birds develop within their eggs. During the incubation period, the eggs must be kept warm so they will hatch.

insecticide—a substance, often composed of chemicals, which is used to kill insects.

logo—a symbol used by a private company or organization to create a public identity.

plumage—the feathered covering of a bird.

predator—an animal that captures, kills, and feeds on other animals.

prey—animals that are hunted for food.

sanctuary—a place where wildlife is safe from hunters.

talon—the claw of a bird of prey, such as a bald eagle.

vermin—an objectionable animal.

zoologist—a scientist who studies animals.

FURTHER READING

Breining, Greg. *Return of the Eagle: How America Saved Its National Symbol*. Helena, MT.: Falcon Publishing Co., 1995.

Carson, Rachel. *Silent Spring*. Boston: Houghton Mifflin Company, 1962.

Collins, Michael. *Carrying the Fire: An Astronaut's Journeys*. New York: Ballantine Books, 1974.

Graham, Frank Jr. "Winged Victory." *Audubon*, July-August 1994.

Lehner, Ernest. *American Symbols*. New York: William Penn Publishing, 1966.

Lemonick, Michael. "Winged Victory." *Time*, July 11, 1994.

Savage, Candace. *Eagles of North America*. New York: Greystone Publishing, 2001.

Schnapper, M. B. *American Symbols: The Seals and Flags of the Fifty States*. Washington: Public Affairs Press, 1974.

INTERNET RESOURCES

Information on the American Bald Eagle
>   http://www.baldeagleinfo.com

Boy Scouts of America
>   http://www.scouting.org

Fraternal Order of Eagles
>   http://www.foe.com

The Great Seal of the United States
>   http://www.greatseal.com

U.S. Fish and Wildlife Service
>   http://www.fws.gov

PICTURE CREDITS

BARRY MORENO has been librarian and historian at the Ellis Island Immigration Museum and the Statue of Liberty National Monument since 1988. He is the author of *The Statue of Liberty Encyclopedia*, which was published by Simon and Schuster in October 2000. He is a native of Los Angeles, California. After graduation from California State University at Los Angeles, where he earned a degree in history, he joined the National Park Service as a seasonal park ranger at the Statue of Liberty; he eventually became the monument's librarian. In his spare time, Barry enjoys reading, writing, and studying foreign languages and grammar. His biography has been included in *Who's Who Among Hispanic Americans*, *The Directory of National Park Service Historians*, *Who's Who in America*, and *The Directory of American Scholars*.

HAL MARCOVITZ is a journalist for *The Morning Call*, a newspaper based in Allentown, Pennsylvania. He has written more than 20 books for young readers. He lives in Chalfont, Pennsylvania, with his wife, Gail, and their daughters, Ashley and Michelle.